A (very brief) History of
SYSTEMIC RACISM:
A Glimpse into Oppression, Inequity, and Inequality of Black People in the United States of America

Written by Chris Valentine

Foreword by CheyOnna Sewell, PhD

Illustrated by Joel Perez

AuthorHouse™
1663 Liberty Drive
Bloomington, IN 47403
www.authorhouse.com
Phone: 1 (833) 262-8899

Because of the dynamic nature of the Internet, any web addresses or links contained in this book may have changed since publication and may no longer be valid. The views expressed in this work are solely those of the author and do not necessarily reflect the views of the publisher, and the publisher hereby disclaims any responsibility for them.

Foreword by CheyOnna Sewell, PhD

This book is printed on acid-free paper.

ISBN: 978-1-6655-0008-1 (sc)
ISBN: 978-1-6655-0009-8 (e)

Print information available on the last page.

Published by AuthorHouse 09/22/2020

authorHOUSE

This book is dedicated to

George W. Lee, Lamar Smith, Willie Edwards Jr., Herbert Lee, Roman Ducksworth Jr., Medgar Evers, Addie Mae Collins, Carol Denise McNair, Carole Robertson, Cynthia Wesley, Virgil Lamar Ware, Louis Allen, Charles Eddie Moore, Henry Hezekiah Dee, James Earl Chaney, Lemuel Penn, Malcolm X, Jimmie Lee Jackson, Oneal Moore, Willie Brewster, Wharlest Jackson, Benjamin Brown, Delano Middleton, Henry Smith, Samuel Hammond Jr., Dr. Martin Luther King Jr., Phillip Pannell, Malice Green, Nicholas Heyward Jr., James Byrd Jr., Amadou Diallo, Bobby Russ, Demetrius DuBose, Timothy DeWayne Thomas Jr., Alberta Spruill, Martin Lee Anderson, Sean Bell, Oscar Grant III, Aiyana Mo'Nay Stanley-Jones, Danroy "DJ" Henry Jr, Reginald Doucet Jr., Ramarley Graham, Trayvon Martin, Rekia Boyd, Shantel Davis, Chavis Carter, Derrick Ambrose Jr., Darnesha Harris, Karvas Gamble Jr, Kayla Moore, Clinton R. Allen, Wayne Arnold Jones, Renisha McBride, Shelly Frey, Yvette Smith, Victor White III, Dontre Hamilton, Tayler Rock, Eric Garner, John Crawford III, Michael Brown, Ezell Ford, Dante Parker, Michelle Cusseaux, Darrien Hunt, Laquan McDonald, Tanisha Anderson, Akai Gurley, Tamir Rice, Rumain Brisbon, Jerame Reid, Matthew Ajibade, Frank Smart, Natasha McKenna, Corey Carter, Tony Robinson, Anthony Hill, Mya Hall, Phillip White, Eric Harris, Walter Scott, Freddie Gray, William Chapman II, Alexia Christian, Kalief Browder, Jonathan Sanders, Freddie Blue, George Mann, Salvado Ellswood, Sandra Bland, Albert Joseph Davis, Darrius Stewart, Billy Ray Davis, Samuel DuBose, Michael Sabbie, Brian Keith Day, Troy Lee Robinson, Christian Taylor, Asshams Pharoah Manley, Felix Kumi, India Kager, La'Vante Biggs, Keith Harrison McLeod, Junior Prosper, Corey Jones, Lamontez Jones, Paterson Brown Jr., Dominic Hutchinson, Anthony Ashford, Jamar Clark, Richard Perkins, Michael Lee Marshall, Nathaniel Harris Pickett Jr., Miguel Espinal, Michael Noel, Kevin Matthews, Bettie Jones, Quintonio LeGrier, Keith Childress Jr., Janet Wilson, Antronie Scott, Wendell Celestine, David Joseph, Randy Nelson, Calin Devonte Roquemore, Dyzhawn Perkins, Christopher Davis, Kionte Spencer, Peter Gaines, Kevin Hicks, Demarcus Semer, Terrill Thomas, Willie Tillman, Alton Sterling, Philando Castile, Joseph Mann, Paul O'neal, Korryn Gaines, Sylville Smith, Tyre King, Terence Crutcher, Bennie Lee Tignor, Alteria Woods, Timothy Caughman, Jordan Edwards, Charleena Lyles, Aaron Bailey, Ronell Foster, Stephon Clark, Antwon Rose II, Botham Jean, Marcus Deon Smith, Jemel Roberson, Willie McCoy, Bradley Blackshire, Pamela Turner, Dominique Clayton, Miles Hall, Troy Hodge, Elijah McClain, Atatiana Jefferson, Christopher Whitfield, Christopher McCorvey, Eric Reason, Michael Lorenzo Dean, Darius Tarver, William Green, Ahmaud Arbery, Manuel Ellis, Breonna Taylor, Monika Diamond, Nina Pop, George Floyd, Dion Johnson, Italia Marie Kelly, David McAtee, Jamel Floyd, Dominique "Rem'Mie" Fells, Riah Milton, Rayshard Brooks, Brayla Stone, Merci Mack, Shaki Peters, Bree Black, and countless others. Rest in Power!

Foreword by CheyOnna Sewell, PhD (Criminology) and Co-Founder of The Yarn Mission

The gravity of the situation surrounding this book is hard to present lightly. I think about how—according to Census data and the Center for Disease Control and Prevention from 2018 to now—over 30% of Black and Indigenous children live in poverty, that Black birthing people are 2 ½ times more likely to die during childbirth than white people, and that Black people are dying from COVID-19 at twice the rate of white people. Systemic racism is killing us. This is not new. Yet, many of you may not know this history and are unaware of the present. I want you to read this book.

We are dying.

"We" being Black Queer Womxn. "We" being those of us who sit at the intersection of multiple marginalized identities. "We" being Black and Indigenous folx bearing the brunt of these systems. "We" being everyone invested in a better present and future. "We" being all, regardless of our understanding of these systems of oppression that permeate our society.

Systemic racism and other oppressive systems means lack of access, blocked opportunities, and heightened risk—Black, queer, Indigenous, and poor people experiencing a disproportionate amount of these disadvantages by merely existing in this society. As directly affected people, we constantly feel the urgency and truth throughout the societal gaslighting that pushes acceptance of these oppressions through meritocracy, personal responsibility, and division. We see the necessity of an ongoing battle against the purposeful indoctrination and disconnection from the history and reality of these harms.

And, we are tired.

I am tired.

As a public and academic educator, I am sensitive to the fact that I am expected to craft a convincing presentation of seemingly objective facts to convey that a real-time genocide of my people and peoples that I love is underway. Additionally, I am adamant that your education should be rooted in the truths compiled and shared by those directly affected by the oppressions you must learn. However, the labor at this point should be carried by the less marginalized, more centered members of our society.

This book is an example of that shift in labor and a much-needed conversation amongst white folx. It is heavily informed by the work and labor of Black folx directly affected by unremedied systemic racism. As such, Chris recognized that this book is a vehicle, an incredible intermediary. He recognized that his labor must also pay tribute to those who are directly affected and frequently dismissed, harmed, and silenced for similar attempts to valiantly educate. Note that "pay tribute" means through actions, support, and monetarily.

This book addresses a wealth of information in a way that stays true to an underlying message that systemic racism harms Black people and is not the fault of Black communities. These messages are bold and necessary.

I hope that you use this book to further ground yourself and others in this knowledge. It cannot be a defense that someone did not know. You have a role in that. Do the work. Let's get free.

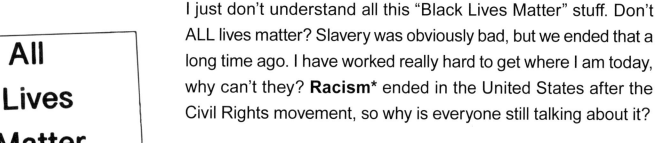

I just don't understand all this "Black Lives Matter" stuff. Don't ALL lives matter? Slavery was obviously bad, but we ended that a long time ago. I have worked really hard to get where I am today, why can't they? **Racism*** ended in the United States after the Civil Rights movement, so why is everyone still talking about it?

Let me tell you a little story about **systemic racism*** in the United States. These are policies and practices purposefully designed into established institutions, which result in the exclusion, prejudice, and discrimination of Black people.

In the beginning, the entire human race originated in Africa. As humans progressed, Africans learned to develop beautiful pieces of art and even pioneered math 25,000 years ago! 12,000 years ago, they began mining for minerals and created stone and metal tools and grew crops. 7,000+ years ago, Africans carved what is possibly the world's first giant sculpture, the Great Sphinx of Giza, and later built the Great Pyramids. They were kings and queens and ruled vast empires, but for many Africans, that changed about 400 years ago when a bunch of politically powerful and influential British people wanted to develop the new world they had conquered, after stealing it from Native people who already lived there. To increase productivity and profits, Colonial settlers decided to employ slave traders who went to Africa and kidnapped Black people and enslaved them. Over the course of 200 years, nearly 12 million Africans were enslaved and taken to the New World, almost 2 million of those would not survive to their destination, and about 400,000 ended up in North America. (Most of the remaining 10 million were shipped to the Caribbean and South America.) The enslaved Africans would do the work that many Colonial white people didn't want to do, and they did it without pay while living in terrible conditions—sick, tired, hungry, and abused.

I know that's awful, but we got rid of slavery, right?

150 years later, in 1776, the people living in the British Colonies were fed up with the way their king was treating them and decided to start their own country—the United States of America. These powerful and influential people created their own government and made new systems and laws that still affect us today. They wrote a breakup letter to King George III, outlining the reasons they were saying goodbye. This letter was called the Declaration of Independence (U.S. 1776).

·The establishment of the United States of America's national government and basic laws would later be written and signed in 1787 as The Constitution of the United States.

The *unanimous* Declaration of the thirteen United States of America

...We hold these truths to be self-evident, that all men are created equal, that they are endowed by their Creator with certain unalienable Rights, that among these are Life, Liberty and the pursuit of Happiness. That to secure these rights, Governments are instituted among Men, deriving their just powers from the consent of the governed--That whenever any Form of Government becomes destructive of these ends, it is the Right of the People to alter or to abolish it, and to institute new Government, laying its foundation on such principles and organizing its power in such form, as to them shall seem most likely to effect their Safety and Happiness. ...it is their right, it is their duty, to throw off such Government, and to provide new Guards for their future security...

It wasn't until another decade later that enslaved Africans were even counted as people, literally. In the 1780s, Southern states felt like they were being cheated out of a voice in Congress because their hostages weren't counting toward their total state population. This argument with the Northern states led to the Three-fifths Compromise of 1787, which would allow Southern states to count 3 out of every 5 enslaved Africans as part of their total population—effectively giving the Southern states ⅓ more seats in the House of Representatives and ⅓ more **electoral votes.*** Having more representation in government allowed Southern states to influence more change in policy making, and more electoral votes meant they had more influence on who would be elected as President of the United States.

The conditions enslaved Africans were living in were so awful that many would rather risk death than to continue being enslaved. One well-known American **abolitionist*** was Harriet Tubman. Tubman was born into slavery but risked her life and escaped the South, running away to the North. After that, she continued to risk her life time and time again as she dodged **Slave Patrols*** (organized groups of armed white men who disciplined enslaved people, and an early form of American police), risking capture and return to slavery, to help nearly 70 enslaved people escape to the North through the Underground Railroad—which wasn't actually a railroad at all but a network of safe houses and secret routes running throughout the United States.

In 1850, The Fugitive Slave Act was passed by Congress (partly because the Southern states now had more seats in the House of Representatives), which required that enslaved people be returned to their "owners" if they were captured in a "free" state. Black people in the North were cautioned to avoid the police because they were empowered to act as kidnappers and slave catchers (very similar to the Slave Patrols). In some cases, rich slave owners offered rewards to private citizens and police officers for the capture, imprisonment, and return of runaway enslaved people.

Just when it was looking like Black people could be enslaved forever, a Civil War broke out between the North and South. This war had a lot to do with the disagreement over whether or not Black people could continue to be enslaved. In 1863, Abraham Lincoln gave a speech called "The Emancipation Proclamation" and said all enslaved people had to be freed. By this time, the nearly 400,000 enslaved Africans originally brought to North America had multiplied into almost 4 million people who were to be set free. The Southern states finally got the message when they lost the Civil War in 1865 and the 13th **Amendment*** was **ratified*** into the Constitution of the United States. Some of the last enslaved people to hear about the abolishment of slavery lived in Texas. They were informed about the abolishment of slavery on June 19th, 1865. In the United States, and especially in Texas, this day is celebrated as a holiday called Juneteenth.

See, things changed for the better, and slaves were set free. And why do you keep calling slaves "enslaved Africans"?

Because words matter and calling enslaved Africans "slaves" makes it sound like they were already slaves in Africa when they were taken to North America, and you're taking away their identity as an African person and replacing it with a situation they've been forced into. It's like saying someone with a disability is disabled, making their whole identity limited to being disabled—they are a complex human with emotions, passions, interests, feelings, friends, family, goals, etc., but they also happen to have a disability, get it? It's only one part of who they are, it's not all of who they are.

That makes sense. I never thought of it like that before.

With the end of the Civil War, the **Black Codes*** were created. These laws restricted African Americans' freedoms and made it so they could be used as a cheap labor force. Some Black Codes required Black people to sign yearly work contracts, and they could be arrested if they refused—which would force them into unpaid labor in prison. These laws significantly limited the freedom of African Americans and made it difficult for them to work and earn a wage. In 1868, the 14th Amendment was ratified and granted citizenship to "all persons born or **naturalized*** in the United States," which included formerly enslaved people who had been freed after the Civil War. It also made the Black Codes illegal. Lawmakers reacted by creating **Jim Crow laws.*** These were state and local laws that encouraged and enforced racial **segregation*** in the South; in many ways, they were very similar laws to the Black Codes. Jim Crow laws existed for almost an entire century before being removed by the Civil Rights Act of 1964 and Voting Rights Act of 1965.

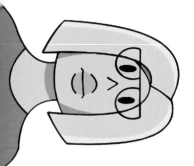

But as you said, Jim Crow laws ended, so now Black people are equal to white people.

You might think so, but Black people weren't truly considered equals to white men because they didn't have the right to vote. The 15th Amendment, ratified in 1870, gave Black men the right to vote. But white policy makers didn't want Black men to vote, so **voter suppression*** tactics were put into place and are still done to this day. Some of the earlier voter suppression techniques included ex-felon **disenfranchisement*** laws, **literacy tests,*** **poll taxes,*** and only allowing Black men to vote if they were landowners (which was extremely difficult for most Black people who had very low, if any, income). Literacy tests were designed to make it difficult for Black men to vote because they typically had little or no education. In many cases, a Black man's white employer would have to grant the Black worker time off work to vote (even today, only 29 states have laws that give registered voters the right to take off time from work to vote on Election Day), and poll taxes were taxes that every adult had to pay in order to vote, regardless of their income. Many Black men couldn't afford these poll taxes, and instead, had to give up their right to vote.

Even after the ratification of the 19th Amendment in 1920, which gave women the right to vote, Black women still had to navigate the same disenfranchisement obstacles that Black men were dealing with up until the passing of the Voting Rights Act of 1965.

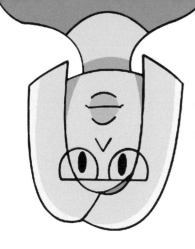

But didn't FDR make it easier for people to get housing loans? That would mean that Black people could own land and would be able to exercise their right to vote.

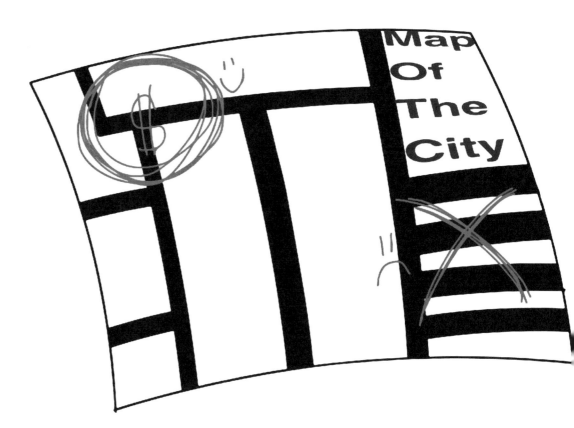

President Franklin Delano Roosevelt founded the Federal Housing Administration through the National Housing Act of 1934, which would regulate interest rates and mortgage terms that it insured, but the restrictions were refused in Black neighborhoods and started a practice known as **redlining.***

These new lending practices increased the number of white people who could afford a down payment on a house and monthly mortgage payments. Black folks, on the other hand, were not given the same treatment and were denied loans to become homeowners. In addition to Black folks being unable to obtain housing loans, redlining marked Black neighborhoods as undesirable and unlikely to appreciate in value—marking the housing in these areas as bad investments.

After World War II, the G.I. Bill, also known as the Servicemen's Readjustment Act of 1944, was passed. The G.I. Bill was a law that was supposed to provide many different benefits to veterans returning after the war. These benefits included letting the VA co-sign and guarantee low-interest mortgages, provide education or training, and more. Sadly, though, these benefits were not extended to most Black people. When the original G.I. Bill ended in 1956, almost 8 million veterans got education or training and 4.3 million home loans were provided, but not to the vast majority of Black veterans, and, in 1947, less than one-tenth of one percent of the G.I. Bill's insured mortgages were for home purchases by Black veterans in some of the biggest cities in the U.S. The G.I. Bill aid that was denied to Black veterans, significantly widened the racial **wealth gap.***

But weren't there public schools that Black kids could go to and get an education? If they just went to school, they could get a good job and be able to afford a house for their families.

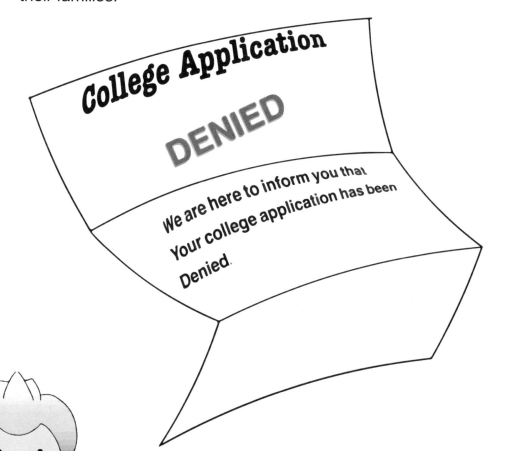

College Application

DENIED

We are here to inform you that
Your college application has been
Denied.

Even though the G.I. Bill was supposed to support veterans trying to attend college, almost all of the Black veterans who applied for college were sent to institutions that were often unaccredited, underfunded, and overwhelmed by so many new students. Tens of thousands of Black veterans who applied for college were turned away because there were too many applicants for the few schools they were allowed to attend. Unable to get the same education as their white counterparts proved to be a huge challenge that was keeping Black people behind, so in 1954, Brown v. Board of Education determined that education segregation was unconstitutional.

Didn't that ruling end an era of "separate but equal"? What more could people want?

NO!

·Before Rosa Parks, Claudette Colvin also refused to give up her bus seat in 1955, but she didn't garner the same kind of attention as Rosa Parks.

What people wanted was to end segregation and Jim Crow laws across the board. In 1955, Rosa Parks refused to give up her seat on a bus in Montgomery, Alabama. Rosa Parks was sitting in a section of the bus not designated for white people only, minding her own business, but when the white section at the front of the bus was too full, Parks was told to move to the back and give up her seat to a white person; she refused to move. Rosa Parks was a civil rights leader and helped start the Montgomery Bus Boycott, pushing Civil Rights issues into the forefront of everyone's mind.

In 1963, Dr. Martin Luther King Jr. gave his famous "I Have a Dream" speech, and many notable Black civil rights leaders and activists gathered people in the streets to protest. They marched to Washington, and, in 1964, the Civil Rights Act legally ended segregation and Jim Crow laws. In the same year, the passing of the 24th Amendment eliminated the Poll Tax, making voting slightly more accessible to Black people.

The Voting Rights Act of 1965 banned the use of literacy tests, authorized the U.S. Attorney General to look into the use of banned poll taxes (yep, they were still being used in some places even after the 24th Amendment was ratified), and gave the federal government oversight of voter registration.

1968 brought about the Fair Housing Act to prohibit discrimination for the sale, rental, and financing of housing based on race, religion, national origin, or sex, and the Housing and Urban Development Act of 1968 increased funding for federal housing programs, gave rent assistance to qualified people, and helped build more low-income housing.

So, there you have it, from slavery to being able to vote, attend schools, and have affordable housing, racism in the United States was completely solved by 1968. But then why are we still having conversations about racism, **inequality,*** and **inequity?***

The 13th Amendment abolished slavery, but there was a loophole that allowed **involuntary servitude*** as a punishment for a crime—a loophole that still exists to this day. That loophole in the 13th Amendment allows prisoners to work for very little or no money (usually no more than 40¢ per hour), effectively becoming an extension of slavery and continuing the tradition of making police an extension of the old Slave Patrols. The 13th Amendment loophole has contributed to the **prison-industrial complex*** we have today. In addition to having public prisons, the United States uses private prisons, which incentivizes our government to fill prison beds. Private prisons can typically offer savings to the government by housing inmates more cheaply than public prisons can. The prison system claims that it wants to help rehabilitate criminals and have them return to society, but a low **recidivism*** rate of released prisoners would eventually cause private prisons to run out of prisoners, which means that private prisons likely want to keep prisoners inside longer and not help them to succeed once released. This cycle is perpetuated even further when private companies who deal with prisons (where they can have goods manufactured for really low wages) create mass media images to reinforce stereotypes that depict people of color, poor people, immigrants, and other groups as criminals. In turn, these companies and private prisons spend lots of money financially backing politicians who have "tough on crime" platforms and will continue making laws that benefit the private prisons and the prison-industrial complex.

Because of this mutually beneficial arrangement between the government and private prisons, the United States, which has roughly 4% of the world's population, has about 25% of the world's entire prison population, according to research data. The **war on drugs*** and other factors involved with the prison-industrial complex have made it so that 1 out of every 3 Black men are expected to go to jail in their lifetime—far disproportionate to white men.

The war on drugs, started by President Richard Nixon in 1971 and institutionalized by President Ronald Reagan in 1980, made it so drug abuse would be considered a criminal issue instead of a health issue. Since 1980, incarceration rates have grown by 300% and drug-related convictions are now the leading contributor to the United States prison population in federal prisons. Studies show that illegal drug use amongst white men and Black men is roughly the same, but Black men are 5 times more likely than white men to be arrested for a drug offense.

Remember the 15th and 19th Amendments? The Amendments that gave Black men and women the right to vote. Well, besides voter suppression, there are disenfranchisement laws (laws that, in many states, make ex-felons lose the right to vote, be employed in certain fields, participate in benefit programs, have parental benefits, travel abroad, or serve on a jury). This ex-felon disenfranchisement means that, even though the 15th Amendment said no one could be excluded from voting based on their race, and the 19th Amendment said no one could be denied the right to vote because of their sex, many Black people aren't allowed to vote on policy changes that affect them, their families, or their communities.

The Department of Housing and Urban Development formed in 1965, and the Fair Housing and Housing and Urban Development Acts of 1968 were supposed to make it easier for Black families to get affordable housing, but redlining and ex-felon laws make it so many Black men and women cannot live in low-income housing. These ex-felon laws also mean that many parents are prohibited from living with their spouses and children in low-income houses, so they are forced to make a difficult decision to leave their families or be homeless so that their kids can have a home.

·In most cases, families must meet certain criteria to qualify for Section 8 housing. These qualifications may include maximum household income, proof of citizenship or eligible immigrant status, no previous eviction history, and no previous criminal conviction record.

Please spare
Some change

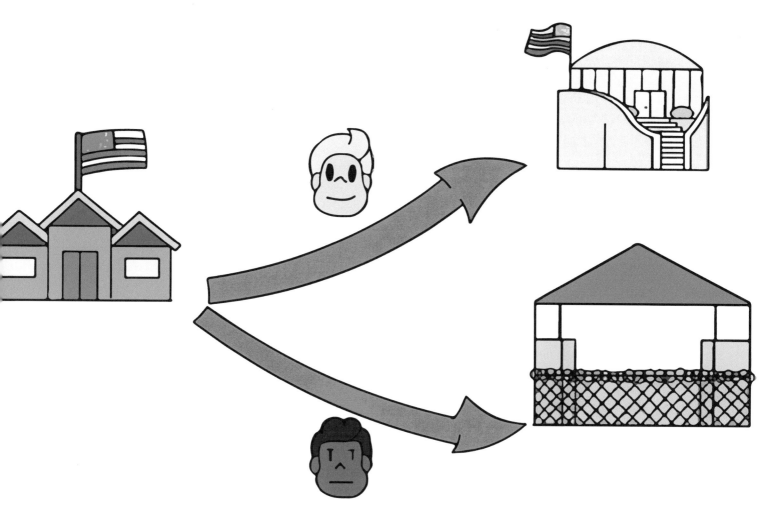

With one less parent in the home, many Black parents are forced to work multiple low-paying jobs just to make ends meet. Their children go to school to get an education, but because of persistent **racial biases*** and **stereotypes,*** Black students are 3 times more likely to be kicked out of school than white students and 2 times more likely to not graduate high school. Students who have been suspended are more likely to be held back a grade or drop out. Less than 70% of Black students graduate high school, and of the students who drop out, 60% will go to prison at some point in their life. This series of events is called the "**school-to-prison pipeline.**"*

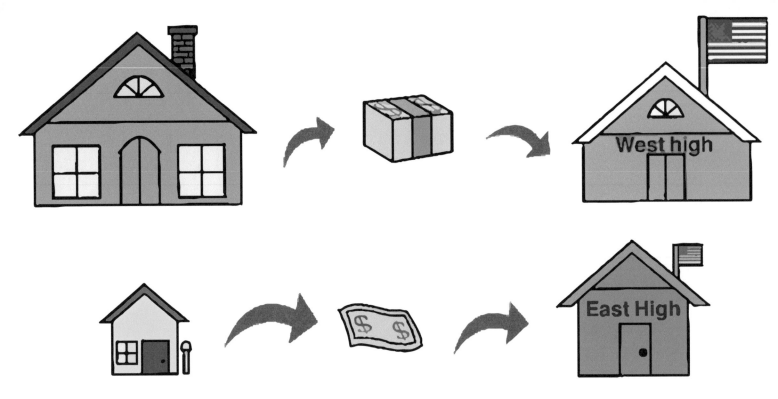

Because of lower income and redlining practices, many Black families are forced to live in lower-income areas. With public schools getting much of their funding from property taxes, schools in these "redlined" districts are less funded than schools in "white" neighborhoods. This lack of funding leads to increased class sizes, teachers who are underpaid, less in-school technology like computer labs, fewer extra-curricular activities, and lower standardized test scores. Lower test scores mean that these public schools are funded even less by the government. All of this further increases the wealth gap and inequality in the United States. In 2017, the median income for white families was around $68,000 per year while the annual median income for Black families was only $40,000, according to the U.S. Census.

As a result of systemic racism in the prison-industrial complex, housing, and education, many people believe these issues are only "Black issues" or that Black people are the cause of their own disadvantage. The #BlackLivesMatter project was organized by three Black women—Alicia Garza, Patrisse Cullors, and Opal Tometi—in response to the acquittal of Trayvon Martin's murderer in 2013. Trayvon Martin, an unarmed 17-year-old Black high school student, was walking when a man called the police on him to report a "suspicious person." Before the police arrived, Trayvon Martin's killer shot him. The point of Black Lives Matter is to remind everyone that Black lives DO matter and to bring people together to end **structural racism*** and **institutional racism*** (two types of systemic racism: the first deals with inequalities rooted in the system, and the latter deals with discrimination that comes from people carrying out the orders of others who are **prejudiced***). Black Lives Matter is a call to address inequities Black people are experiencing due to systemic racism. If you reply with, "All Lives Matter," you are shifting the conversation away from those inequities and making the story about yourself. Black Lives Matter doesn't mean that other lives don't matter or that ONLY Black Lives Matter, it means that Black Lives Matter too.

Oh wow! I had no idea. What can I do to help?

The most important thing you can do is to educate yourself and others about these issues. While you're learning more about systemic racism, you can help by donating time and/or money, signing a petition, helping people in need, supporting causes and organizations better equipped to deal with these issues head-on, vote, and recognize and understand your **privileges*** (which doesn't mean you don't have hardships, it just means the advantages you have because of your skin color, sex, sexual orientation, physical ability, income, etc. don't create additional obstacles for you) and how to use them to help make a better country. We need to do more to help increase awareness of systemic racism, institutional racism, structural racism, and **individual racism*/interpersonal racism*** to address these issues at their core. This doesn't just include the prison-industrial complex; it also includes systemic racism in education, housing, public health, hiring discrimination, and more!

And this is just the surface of inequality, inequity, and racism still prevalent in the United States right now. There is so much more to talk about, but this (very brief) history of systemic racism is just a short book to help get you started. I sincerely wish you the best of luck as you go forth and help change the world!

For more information and links to additional resources, or to further the discussion, please visit www.thechrisvalentine.com or join me on Facebook or Instagram at @thechrisvalentine.

Glossary

- **Abolitionist:** a person who wants to abolish, or get rid of, systemic and institutionalized practices and organizations that oppress people. Harriet Tubman wanted to abolish slavery.
- **Amendment:** a change (to The Constitution of the United States) that becomes a law. The Constitution of the United States is a set of rules that all other laws and mandates are examined against to determine if they are "constitutional" or "unconstitutional." Laws that are determined to be "unconstitutional" must be changed so they don't violate anyone's constitutional rights. Well-known examples of amendments to The Constitution would include The Bill of Rights (The first 10 amendments to The Constitution), which include freedom of expression and religion, the right to bearing arms, and several rights for people accused of crimes.
- **Disenfranchisement:** to have the right to vote (or another right) taken away.
- **Electoral Votes:** the votes cast by the electoral college for a presidential election.
- **Individual Racism:** a belief that your own race is somehow superior to someone else's race.
- **Inequality:** someone doesn't have the same (equal) rights, opportunities, privileges, or status as someone else.
- **Inequity:** someone doesn't have the same fairness or justice as someone else.
- **Institutional Racism:** racism that takes the form of rules, regulations, practices, standards, or customs of organizations. This could be related to employers or, in the case of this book, the institutions of government—Bureau of Prisons, Education Department, etc.
- **Interpersonal Racism:** is when a person brings racism into a situation where another person is involved. If individual racism is thinking your race makes you superior, then interpersonal racism can be thought of as if you then told someone else that your race makes you superior to them.

- **Involuntary Servitude:** when someone is legally and constitutionally working but to the benefit of someone else, and not themselves.
- **Literacy Tests:** tests used to determine if a potential voter was capable of reading before being allowed to cast a vote. In practice, literacy tests were often designed to be confusing or would have unrealistic expectations of the person taking the test—such as being able to name every judge in their county or state.
- **Naturalized:** when an immigrant (someone not born in the U.S.) is granted citizenship.
- **Poll Taxes:** taxes that people had to pay to be allowed to vote, regardless of income or availability of resources.
- **Prejudiced:** when someone has an opinion about another person that isn't based on actual experiences or facts. Prejudices are usually negative attitudes toward someone based on that person's social group, such as not liking someone who is poor or lives in a "bad" neighborhood.
- **Prison-Industrial Complex:** created when industries that benefit from prisons have overlapping interests with the government, creating a mutually beneficial relationship that encourages putting more people in prison and keeping them there.
- **Privileges:** advantages or special rights that someone has just because they belong to a specific group. We often hear of white privilege, which refers to the benefits white people have because of the color of their skin. Having privilege doesn't mean that you don't have troubles, it means that the group you belong to doesn't create more troubles for you. Other examples of privilege include privileges of being a man, identifying as heterosexual, being able-bodied, having a job, belonging to a specific religion, identifying as the sex you are born into, being in good health, being fit or thin, etc. You can usually identify your privileges as being parts of your identity that you don't have to think about on a regular basis because they don't negatively impact your experiences in life.

- **Racial Biases:** a form of unconscious bias (stereotypes about certain people that someone forms without conscious awareness) that is specifically about race. People can develop racial biases by seeing/hearing what is portrayed in the media about specific groups of people or by growing up hearing negative (or positive) comments from family regarding a group of people.

- **Racism:** can be the belief, attitude, or behaviors that favor one race (or skin color) over another, by an individual, or a system of institutionalized power that, in the context of this book, gives white people decision/policy making power over Black people.

- **Ratified:** to sign something or give something formal consent to make it official. For an amendment to be ratified into The Constitution means it was signed into law.

- **Redlining:** a practice of dividing cities by neighborhoods and labeling them as desirable, declining, or hazardous, primarily based on each neighborhood's demographics.

- **School-to-Prison Pipeline:** a national trend where children go directly from being in school to being in juvenile detention or the criminal justice systems. After the Columbine school shooting on April 20, 1999, many schools began having police officers in the building. Data shows that this has not reduced the number of school shootings but has significantly increased the number of students being arrested and put in juvenile detention or prison, effectively increasing the school-to-prison pipeline in the U.S.

- **Segregation:** the separation of a minority group of people from the majority, based on race, ethnicity, religion, etc.

- **Slave Patrols:** organized groups of armed white men who monitored and enforced discipline upon enslaved people, and one of the earliest forms of American police.

- **Stereotypes:** widely accepted beliefs about specific groups of people. Some examples of stereotypes still prevalent today would include the stereotype that women are better at baking than men or that men are harder workers than women.
- **Structural Racism:** racism that has become a part of social systems, such as when history in school is taught primarily from a white perspective. Structural racism is also seen in political and economic systems.
- **Systemic Racism:** policies and practices purposefully designed into established institutions, which result in the exclusion, prejudice, and discrimination of a minority group (in the context of this book, Black people).
- **Unalienable Rights:** (or inalienable rights) are rights that cannot be taken away or denied.
- **Voter Suppression:** strategies and tactics used to keep certain people from being able to vote.
- **War on Drugs:** an initiative aimed at reducing the illegal drug usage and trade in the United States that disproportionately affects people of color.
- **Wealth Gap:** the unequal distribution of wealth between different groups of people. This book is specifically talking about the unequal distribution of wealth between Black people and white people.

Notes

Roos, Dave. "Why Was the Electoral College Created?" History. A&E Television Networks, July 15, 2019. https://www.history.com/news/electoral-college-founding-fathers-constitutional-convention

The Editors of Encyclopaedia Britannica, ed. "Three-Fifths Compromise." Encyclopædia Britannica. Encyclopædia Britannica, Inc., June 26, 2020. https://www.britannica.com/topic/three-fifths-compromise

Hansen, Chelsea. "Slave Patrols: An Early Form of American Policing." National Law Enforcement Museum, July 10, 2019. https://lawenforcementmuseum.org/2019/07/10/slave-patrols-an-early-form-of-american-policing/

The Editors of Encyclopaedia Britannica. "Fugitive Slave Acts." Encyclopædia Britannica. Encyclopædia Britannica, Inc., July 23, 2020. https://www.britannica.com/event/Fugitive-Slave-Acts

U.S. Const. Amend. XIII, § 1

U.S. Const. Amend. XIV, § 1

U.S. Const. Amend. XV, § 1

U.S. Const. Amend. XIX

U.S. Const. Amend. XXIV, § 1

History.com Editors, ed. "Black Codes." HISTORY. A&E Television Networks, June 1, 2010. https://www.history.com/topics/black-history/black-codes

History.com Editors, ed. "Jim Crow Laws." HISTORY A&E Television Networks, February 28, 2018. https://www.history.com/topics/early-20th-century-us/jim-crow-laws

Urofsky, Melvin I. "Jim Crow Law." Encyclopædia Britannica. Encyclopædia Britannica, Inc., July 23, 2020. https://www.britannica.com/event/Jim-Crow-law

Smithsonian, ed. "White Only: Jim Crow in America" Smithsonian. National Museum of American History. https://americanhistory.si.edu/brown/history/1-segregated/white-only-1.html

Axelrod Ph.D., Alan. The Complete Texts of American History & Science. New York, NY: The Berkley Publishing Group, 2003.

Irving, Debby. Waking up White: and Finding Myself in the Story of Race. Cambridge, MA: Elephant Room Press, 2014.

Tatum, Beverly Daniel. Why Are All the Black Kids Sitting Together in the Cafeteria?: and Other Conversations about Race. New York, NY: Basic Books, 2017.

Oluo, Ijeoma. So You Want to Talk about Race. New York, NY: Seal Press, 2020.

Khan-Cullors, Patrisse, and Asha Bandele. WHEN THEY CALL YOU A TERRORIST: A Story of Black Lives Matter, Love, Activism, and the Power to Change the World. New York, NY: WEDNESDAY Books, 2020.

Erb, Kelly Phillips. "For Election Day, A History of The Poll Tax in America." Forbes. Forbes Magazine, November 5, 2018. https://www.forbes.com/sites/kellyphillipserb/2018/11/05/just-before-the-elections-a-history-of-the-poll-tax-in-america/

Chung, Jean. "Felony Disenfranchisement: A Primer." The Sentencing Project, June 27, 2019. https://www.sentencingproject.org/publications/felony-disenfranchisement-a-primer/

"National Housing Act of 1934." Encyclopedia of the Great Depression. Encyclopedia.com, July 14, 2020. https://www.encyclopedia.com/economics/encyclopedias-almanacs-transcripts-and-maps/national-housing-act-1934

"Civil Rights Act of 1964." West's Encyclopedia of American Law. Encyclopedia.com, July 15, 2020. https://www.encyclopedia.com/law/encyclopedias-almanacs-transcripts-and-maps/civil-rights-act-1964

senate.gov. "Landmark Legislation: The Civil Rights Act of 1964." U.S. Senate: Landmark Legislation: The Civil Rights Act of 1964, January 12, 2017. https://www.senate.gov/artandhistory/history/common/generic/CivilRightsAct1964.htm

History.com Editors. "Voting Rights Act of 1965." HISTORY. A&E Television Networks, November 9, 2009. https://www.history.com/topics/black-history/voting-rights-act

History.com Editors. "Brown v. Board of Education." History.com. A&E Television Networks, October 27, 2009. https://www.history.com/topics/black-history/brown-v-board-of-education-of-topeka

Blakemore, Erin. "How the GI Bill's Promise Was Denied to a Million Black WWII Veterans." History.com. A&E Television Networks, June 21, 2019. https://www.history.com/news/gi-bill-black-wwii-veterans-benefits

Adams, Michelle. "The Unfulfilled Promise of the Fair Housing Act." The New Yorker, April 11, 2018. https://www.newyorker.com/news/news-desk/the-unfulfilled-promise-of-the-fair-housing-act

Schlosser, Eric. "The Prison-Industrial Complex." The Atlantic. Atlantic Media Company, 1998. https://www.theatlantic.com/magazine/archive/1998/12/the-prison-industrial-complex/304669/

Nelson, Libby, and Dara Lind. "The School to Prison Pipeline, Explained" Justice Policy Institute, February 24, 2015. http://www.justicepolicy.org/news/8775

History.com Editors. "War on Drugs." HISTORY. A&E Television Networks, May 31, 2017. https://www.history.com/topics/crime/the-war-on-drugs

Lynch, Matthew. "A Guide to Ending the Crisis Among Young Black Males," April 6, 2017. https://www.theedadvocate.org/guide-ending-crisis-among-young-black-males/

Department of Housing and Urban Development. "HUD Media Kit: LBJ Presidential Library." Media Kit | Department of Housing and Urban Development (HUD). LBJ Presidential Library. http://www.lbjlibrary.org/mediakits/hud/

History.com Editors. "Voting Rights Act of 1965." HISTORY. A&E Television Networks, November 9, 2009. https://www.history.com/topics/black-history/voting-rights-act

The People's School of DC Editors. "Housing Discrimination." The People's School of DC, September 24, 2019. https://peoplesschooldc.wordpress.com/housing-discrimination-2/

U.S. Census Bureau. Real Median Household Income by Race and Hispanic Origin: 1967 to 2007. Census.gov. U.S. Census Bureau, Current Population Survey, 2018. https://www.census.gov/content/dam/Census/library/visualizations/2018/demo/p60-263/figure1.pdf

Blakemore, Erin. "How the GI Bill's Promise Was Denied to a Million Black WWII Veterans." HISTORY. A&E Television Networks, June 21, 2019. https://www.history.com/news/gi-bill-black-wwii-veterans-benefits

Katznelson, Ira. When Affirmative Action Was White: An Untold History of Racial Inequality in Twentieth-Century America. New York, NY: W.W. Norton, 2006.

U.S. Dept of Defense. "75 Years of the GI Bill: How Transformative It's Been." U.S. DEPARTMENT OF DEFENSE, January 9, 2019. https://www.defense.gov/Explore/Features/story/Article/1727086/75-years-of-the-gi-bill-how-transformative-its-been/

Baker, Peter C. "The Tragic, Forgotten History of Black Military Veterans." The New Yorker, November 27, 2016. https://www.newyorker.com/news/news-desk/the-tragic-forgotten-history-of-black-military-veterans

JUNETEENTH, .com. "History of Juneteenth," 1996. https://www.juneteenth.com/history.htm

About the Author

Chris Valentine—data analyst by day, artist by night—has a unique ability to take overwhelming amounts of information (literally hundreds of years of American History, in the case of this book) and break it down into small bits that fit nicely together to tell a complete story. Chris is certainly not an expert about racism, but he is someone who cares deeply about fighting discrimination based on peoples' fundamental essence that they cannot choose or change. Chris is a cis-gender, white, gay man who is heartbroken, angry, and sick over the inequities perpetrated against people every day. Even though Chris cannot walk in the shoes of Black people, he is empathetic to their experience and is working hard to be an anti-racist ally. As Chris continues his anti-racist journey, he hopes to help others start or continue their journeys too.

Join Chris on Instagram or Facebook at @thechrisvalentine.

Printed in the United States
By Bookmasters